Saint Anthony

Novena and Prayers

❧

By

Mary Mark Wickenhiser, FSP

Pauline
BOOKS & MEDIA

Boston

Nihil Obstat: Rev. John E. Sassani

Imprimatur: ✠ Most Rev. Richard G. Lennon
Apostolic Administrator of
the Archdiocese of Boston
March 17, 2003

ISBN 0-8198-7072-2

Cover art: Tracy Christianson

Texts of the New Testament used in this work are taken from *The St. Paul Catholic Edition of the New Testament,* translated by Mark A. Wauck. Copyright © 1992, Society of St. Paul. All rights reserved.

Texts of the Psalms used in this work are translated by Manuel Miguens. Copyright © 1995, Daughters of St. Paul.

Published in the U.S.A. by Pauline Books & Media, 50 Saint Pauls Avenue, Boston, MA 02130-3491. www.pauline.org.

Printed in the U.S.A.

Pauline Books & Media is the publishing house of the Daughters of St. Paul, an international congregation of women religious serving the Church with the communications media.

5 6 7 8 9 10   23 22 21 20 19

Contents

What Is a Novena? ---------------------- 5

St. Anthony ---------------------------- 9

Morning Prayer --------------------- 12

Novena to St. Anthony ------------ 18

Prayers for Various Needs --------- 31

Evening Prayer --------------------- 41

What Is a Novena?

The Catholic tradition of praying novenas has its roots in the earliest days of the Church. In the Acts of the Apostles we read that after the ascension of Jesus, the apostles returned to Jerusalem, to the upper room, where "They all devoted themselves single-mindedly to prayer, along with some women and Mary the Mother of Jesus and his brothers" (Acts 1:14). Jesus had instructed his disciples to wait for the coming of the Holy Spirit, and on the day of Pentecost, the Spirit of the Lord came to them. This prayer of the first Christian community was the first "novena." Based on this, Christians have always prayed for various needs, trusting that God both hears and answers prayer.

The word "novena" is derived from the Latin term *novem*, meaning nine. In biblical times numbers held deep symbolism for people. The number "three," for example, symbolized perfection, fullness, completeness. The number nine—three times three—symbolized perfection times perfection. Novenas developed because it was thought that—symbolically speaking—nine days represented the perfect amount of time to pray. The ancient Greeks and Romans had the custom of mourning for nine days after a death. The early Christian Church offered Mass for the deceased for nine consecutive days. During the Middle Ages novenas in preparation for solemn feasts became popular, as did novenas to particular saints.

Whether a novena is made solemnly—in a parish church in preparation for a feastday—or in the privacy of one's home, as Christians we never really pray alone. Through the waters of Baptism we have become members of the body of Christ and are thereby united to every other member of Christ's Mystical Body. When we pray, we are spiritually united with all the other members.

Just as we pray for each other while here on earth, those who have gone before us and are united with God in heaven can pray for us and intercede for us as well. We Catholics use the term "communion of saints" to refer to this exchange of spiritual help among the members of the Church on earth, those who have died and are being purified, and the saints in heaven.

While nothing can replace the celebration of Mass and the sacraments as the Church's highest form of prayer, devotions have a special place in Catholic life. Devotions such as the Stations of the Cross can help us enter into the sufferings of Jesus and give us an understanding of his personal love for us. The mysteries of the rosary can draw us into meditating on the lives of Jesus and Mary. Devotions to the saints can help us witness to our faith and encourage us in our commitment to lead lives of holiness and service as they did.

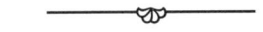

How to use this booklet

The morning and evening prayers are modeled on the Liturgy of the Hours, following its pattern of psalms, scripture readings and intercessions.

We suggest that during the novena you make time in your schedule to pray the morning prayer and evening prayer. If you are able, try to also set aside a time during the day when you can pray the novena and any other particular prayer(s) you have chosen. Or you can recite the devotional prayers at the conclusion of the morning or evening prayer. What is important is to pray with expectant faith and confidence in a loving God who will answer our prayers in the way that will most benefit us. The Lord "satisfies the thirsty, and the hungry he fills with good things" (Ps 107:9).

St. Anthony

Almost 800 years after his death, Anthony remains a very popular saint. Born in Lisbon, Portugal, in 1195, he was baptized Fernando and later entered the Canons Regular of St. Augustine. He spent eight years at a monastery in Coimbra, studied Scripture and was ordained a priest in 1220. When the bodies of some Franciscans who had been martyred in Morocco were brought to Coimbra for burial, Fernando was deeply moved by their heroic witness. He transferred to the Franciscans, changed his name to Anthony, and went to Morocco. But he became sick there and soon had to return to Europe. In 1221 Anthony attended the general chapter of the Franciscans in Assisi, where he met St. Francis. Then Anthony went to live as a hermit at Montepaolo. No one realized his gifts, but that would soon change.

At an ordination the following year, Anthony was unexpectedly invited to preach. Although he was unknown and unprepared, he spoke so eloquently that he astonished everyone there. His superiors then sent him on mission, to preach the Word of God to the people. For the next several years Anthony traveled through northern Italy and southern France, drawing great crowds who wanted to hear this charismatic young friar. He brought back to the Catholic faith many people who had joined heretical sects known as Waldensians and Albigensians. But not everyone listened to him. Legend has it that in one town, where the people spurned him, Anthony went to the river and preached to an attentive audience of fish!

Anthony returned to Italy and became provincial of the Roman province. He was also the first Franciscan teacher of theology, so learned that St. Francis referred to him as "my bishop." In 1227 Anthony went to Padua, where he continued his work of preaching the Word of God. He had a charismatic gift for healing and he became known for the miraculous healings that followed on his prayers.

Anthony's health had never been robust since his illness in Africa. Some historians think he had a combination of dropsy and asthma or hepatitis. Whatever the ailment, it made traveling very painful. Although he was barely thirty-six years old, he died on June 13, 1231, worn out from fatigue, poverty, and penance. People received so many miracles through his intercession that he was popularly acclaimed a saint. On May 30, 1232, Pope Gregory IX canonized him. In 1946 Pope Pius XII declared Anthony a doctor of the Church.

Anthony's life holds great relevance for us today. His love and care for the needy gave rise to the Franciscan tradition of St. Anthony's bread. Anthony based his preaching on Sacred Scripture, and used it constantly in his prayer. He stressed that everyone is called to holiness, anticipating the teaching of Vatican II. Although he is popularly known as the finder of lost objects, Anthony's concern is not so much for finding lost things as for finding those who have lost their path to God. A story from his life illustrates this. A novice in his community ran away, taking with him Anthony's book of psalms. Anthony prayed fervently that he would find the book, which was very precious to him because it had all his notes for teaching, but he also prayed that the thief would have a change of heart. Soon enough the runaway novice not only returned Anthony's book, but also rejoined the community.

Marianne Lorraine Trouvé, FSP

Morning Prayer

Morning prayer is a time to give praise and thanks to God, to remind ourselves that he is the source of all beauty and goodness. Lifting one's heart and mind to God in the early hours of the day puts one's life into perspective: God is our loving Creator who watches over us with tenderness and is always ready to embrace us with his compassion and mercy.

While at prayer, try to create a prayerful atmosphere, perhaps with a burning candle to remind you that Christ is the light who illumines your daily path, an open Bible to remind you that the Lord is always present, a crucifix to remind you of the depths of God's love for you. Soft music can also contribute to a serene and prayerful mood.

If a quiet place is not available, or if you pray as you commute to and from work, remember that the God who loves you is present everywhere and hears your prayer no matter the setting.

It is good to give thanks and praise the Lord our
    God,
to proclaim his love in the morning.
Glory to the Father, and to the Son, and to the
    Holy Spirit,
as it was in the beginning, is now, and will be
    forever. Amen.

Psalm 104

Glory and praise to our God, forever.

Bless the LORD, my soul.
LORD my God, how great you are.
You are robed in splendor and majesty,
clothed in light as a cloak,
you spread out the heavens like a tent,
set the timbers for your lodgings on the waters,
make the clouds your chariot,
and you ride on the wings of the wind.
You establish the winds as your messengers,
flames of fire as your ministers.
You fixed the foundations of the earth
so that it shall not be moved for an eternity
    of eternities.
I will sing to the LORD as long as I live,
sing psalms to my God while I still have life.

May this meditation of mine be pleasing to him,
for I rejoice in the LORD.
Bless the LORD, my soul. Alleluia.

Glory to the Father....

Psalm 34

*Praise and thanks to our God
who upholds us in time of distress.*

I will bless the LORD at all times;
his praise is ever on my lips.
It is in the LORD that my soul shall boast.
The humble shall hear of it and rejoice.
Join me in celebrating the greatness of the LORD,
and let us extol his name together.
I sought the LORD and he answered me;
he delivered me from all my fears.
Those who gazed on him were radiant with joy
and their faces were not made to blush.
The afflicted ones cried out and the LORD heard,
and saved them from all their troubles.

Glory to the Father....

The Word of God

Matthew 5:14–16

As followers of Jesus Christ, we are called to focus on our talents and good qualities, not just our failings and inadequacies. Taking time to reflect on our gifts also allows us the opportunity to discern how we can best use our talents to serve the kingdom of Christ here on earth.

You are the light of the world.
A city cannot be hidden,
if it is set atop a mountain.
Nor do you light a lamp and set it beneath
   a bushel;
you set it on the lampstand, instead,
so it gives light to everyone in the house.
Let your light so shine before men
that they will see your good works
and glorify your Father in Heaven.

Your word, Lord, gives joy to my heart!

From prayer one draws the strength needed to meet the challenges of daily life as a committed follower of Jesus Christ, and as such to be a living sign of the Lord's loving presence in the world.

Intercessions

*H*eavenly Father, I rejoice in the gift of a new day, and with joy in your loving presence seek your grace and blessing:

Response: *Lord, guide me along the right path.*

Inspire my thoughts, words, and actions, so that all I do and say may be pleasing to you and serve your kingdom here on earth. **R.**

Help me to use my gifts and talents to generously serve the needs of others. **R.**

Grant that I may spend this day in joy of spirit and peace of mind. **R.**

Be with me today that I may recognize the opportunities to let my light shine so that others may glorify your name. **R.**

Conclude your intercessions by praying to our Heavenly Father in the words Jesus taught us:

Our Father, who art in heaven, hallowed be thy name; thy kingdom come; they will be done on earth as it is in heaven. Give us this day our daily bread, and forgive us our trespasses, as we forgive those who trespass against us, and lead us not into temptation, but deliver us from evil. Amen.

Closing Prayer

*L*ord our God, be my strength and my hope this day. Use me as an instrument of your love in the lives of those I meet today. I ask this and all things in the name of Jesus, your Son. Amen.

Let us praise the Lord.
And give him thanks.

Novena to St. Anthony

The Thirteen Tuesdays
in Honor of St. Anthony

As a spiritual preparation for the feast of St. Anthony it is customary to pray the Thirteen Tuesdays. This prayer begins in March and ends on the Tuesday before June 13.

Each day there is a Scripture passage to consider, a brief extract from the Sermons of St. Anthony[1] to ponder, and a concluding prayer. These reflections highlight the fruits of the Holy Spirit (Gal 5:22–23), the spiritual qualities or virtues that the Holy Spirit desires to form in us as he did in the heart of St. Anthony.

---

1. The excerpts from St. Anthony's sermons are taken from Claude M. Jarmak, O.F.M. Conv., *If You Seek Miracles: Reflections of St. Anthony of Padua* (Padua: Edizioni Messaggero Padova, 1998), and from Paul Spilsbury, trans. *The Sermons of St. Anthony of Padua,* found online at www.franciscan-2archive.org/antonius/opera/ant-hd00.html.

First Tuesday
Devotion to St. Anthony

Consider

"Ask! and it shall be given to you;
seek! and you shall find;
knock! and it shall be opened to you.
For everyone who asks, will receive,
and whoever seeks, will find,
and to those who knock, it shall be opened." (Mt 7:7–8)

Ponder

For I shall rejoice over your well-being as though it were my own. My glory shall be your consolation and exultation, and yours shall be mine. (Sermons of St. Anthony)

Pray

Almighty and eternal God, you have given St. Anthony to your people as an outstanding preacher, and bestowed on him the gift of miraculous powers. With his help may we follow the way of the Gospel and receive the assistance of your grace in time of need. In your mercy grant that what we seek through St. Anthony's merits we may receive through his intercession *(mention your request)*. We ask this through Jesus Christ your Son, our Lord. Amen.

Second Tuesday
Charity

Consider

Above all be constant in your love for one another, because love covers a multitude of sins. Be hospitable to each other without complaining. To the extent that each of you has received a gift, use it to serve one another. (1 Pt 4:8–11)

Ponder

One and the same love embraces both God and neighbor, and this love is the Holy Spirit, for God is love. (Sermons of St. Anthony)

Pray *(see page 19)*

Third Tuesday

Joy

Consider

May God, the source of hope, fill you with all joy and peace through your belief in him, so that you will overflow with hope by the power of the Holy Spirit. (Rom 15:13)

Ponder

When we rejoice our joy and laughter should echo that of the Virgin Mother whose joy and enthusiasm were expressed in her song of praise: "My being proclaims the greatness of the Lord and my spirit finds joy in God, my savior." (Sermons of St. Anthony)

Pray *(see page 19)*

Fourth Tuesday

Peace

Consider

Let the peace of Christ rule in your hearts, the peace to which you were called in one body, and be thankful. Let the word of Christ dwell in you richly. Whatever you do, whether in word or deed, do it in the name of Jesus the Lord. (Col 3:15–17)

Ponder

Put aside the cares and distractions of this life. Enter into the house of your conscience and close the door of your five senses. You will then find peace in wisdom because you will be able to give yourself to the contemplation of heavenly things. (Sermons of St. Anthony)

Pray *(see page 19)*

Fifth Tuesday
Patience

Consider

The Spirit itself bears witness with our spirit that we are God's children. And if we are children, then we are also heirs—heirs of God, co-heirs with Christ, if we suffer with him so as to be glorified with him as well.

I consider that the sufferings of the present time simply do not compare with the glory to come, which will be revealed to us. (Rom 8:16–18)

Ponder

Follow after Christ and carry your cross for your salvation, as Christ carried his cross for your redemption. (Sermons of St. Anthony)

Pray *(see page 19)*

Sixth Tuesday
Kindness

Consider

Everyone should be quick to listen, but slow to speak and slow to anger. For a person's anger does not achieve the righteousness God demands. Lay aside, therefore, every evil excess and humbly accept the word that has been planted in you and is able to save your soul. (Jas 1:19–21)

Ponder

Nature itself restrains the tongue behind two enclosures so that it will not roam about freely. These two enclosures are the teeth and the lips. This was done to teach us that a word should not leave the mouth except with utmost caution. Be attentive so that you guard the tongue not only with the enclosure of teeth, but also with the enclosure of the lips. A person can be said to have both enclosures guarded if he avoids both criticism and empty flattery. (Sermons of St. Anthony)

Pray (see page 19)

Seventh Tuesday
Goodness

Consider

Continually offer through [Jesus] a sacrifice of praise to God, the fruit of lips that acknowledge his name. Do not forget to do good and to share what you have, for these are the sacrifices which are pleasing to God. (Heb 13:15–16)

Ponder

It is only in hardship that we come to know whether we have made real progress in goodness. (Sermons of St. Anthony)

Pray *(see page 19)*

Eighth Tuesday
Generosity

Consider

By grace you have been saved through faith; and this was God's gift, it did not come from you, not from your own efforts, so that no one would boast. For we are God's handiwork, created in Christ Jesus for the purpose of carrying out those good works for which God prepared us beforehand, so that we might lead our lives in the performance of good works. (Eph 2:8–10)

Ponder

What we hold in our hearts as good, we must show outwardly also in our good deeds; what we have tasted of God in prayer must be reflected in our love for neighbor. (Sermons of St. Anthony)

Pray *(see page 19)*

Ninth Tuesday
Gentleness

Consider

As God's chosen ones, holy and beloved, clothe yourselves with true compassion, kindness, humility, gentleness, patience; bear with one another and forgive each other if anyone has a grievance against someone else. Just as the Lord forgave you, you too should do the same. (Col 3:12–13)

Ponder

As the sail drives a ship, so let compassion lead you to care for others. (Sermons of St. Anthony)

Pray (see page 19)

Tenth Tuesday
Faithfulness

Consider

Rejoice always, pray constantly, give thanks no matter what happens, for this is God's will for you in Christ Jesus.

May the God of peace himself sanctify you completely, and may your spirit, soul, and body be kept sound and blameless for the coming our Lord Jesus Christ. He who calls you is faithful, and he will do it! (1 Thes 5:16, 17, 18, 23–24)

Ponder

When the Holy Spirit enters the soul he clothes it with power from on high. From on high he gives strength to the weary, fortitude and power to the weak; strength that it may rise up, fortitude that it may not fail in time of temptation, power that it may persevere unto the end. (Sermons of St. Anthony)

Pray *(see page 19)*

Eleventh Tuesday
Modesty

Consider

Humble yourselves beneath God's mighty hand so that he will exalt you at the proper time; cast all your cares on him, because he cares for you. (1 Pt 5:6–7)

Ponder

Just as the roots support and nourish the tree, so does humility support and nourish the soul. The spirit of humility is sweeter than honey, and those who nourish themselves with this honey produce sweet fruit. (Sermons of St. Anthony)

Pray *(see page 19)*

Twelfth Tuesday
Self-Control

Consider

Take up God's armor.... Gird your loins with truth and put on the breastplate of righteousness! Put on your feet the boots of preparedness for the good news! And along with all this take up the shield of the faith, with which you will be able to extinguish all the flaming arrows of the Evil One. Take the helmet of salvation and the sword of the Spirit, which is the word of God. (Eph 6:13–18)

Ponder

Battles are usually fought in a field or on a plain. In the world there is a continuous battle, with attacks launched by the flesh, the world, and the devil. A good solid holiness is indispensable for anyone desiring to come away victorious amid all the dangers of this struggle. (Sermons of St. Anthony)

Pray *(see page 19)*

Thirteenth Tuesday
Chastity

Consider

Do you not know that your bodies are Temples of the Holy Spirit within you, who comes to you from God, and that you do not belong to yourselves? You were bought for a price, so glorify God in your bodies. (1 Cor 6:19–20)

Ponder

All the graces of God in this present life are only a little drop in comparison with his eternal recompense. (Sermons of St. Anthony)

Pray (see page 19)

Prayers for Various Needs

Any one of the following prayers may be used according to the intention for the novena.

Prayer for Every Need

*H*eavenly Father, ever praised and glorified in your servant St. Anthony, whose intercessory power even today is a sign of your divine grace always at work in the world.

During his life on earth you gifted your servant Anthony with special favors and granted that even from heaven he should continue to intercede for those who seek his help.

With confidence in your compassionate love, O Lord, I offer this prayer through the intercession of St. Anthony and ask that you grant my request *(special intention)*.

St. Anthony, pray for me and all my loved ones that we may obtain the graces we need to be faithful followers of Jesus: to love God above all things; to love our neighbor as ourselves; to share with the poor unselfishly. Teach me, holy St. Anthony, to walk the path of faith and to proclaim that faith in word and action until the day I can join you and all the saints to praise God forever in heaven.

I ask these and all spiritual blessings, in the name of the Father, and of the Son, and of the Holy Spirit. Amen.

For Guidance and Protection

Glorious St. Anthony, friend of all who invoke your name, accept the sincerity of my devotion and receive me under your protection. Obtain for me the graces I need to keep Jesus always in my heart. Be my guide today and every day; teach me compassion so that I might look beyond my own wants and, in love, reach out to those who are alone and in need. Pray that I may let the Lord use me as he used you, so that I can be an instrument of his love in the world, and proclaim the Gospel message in word and deed.

Our Father, who art in heaven, hallowed be thy name; thy kingdom come; thy will be done on earth as it is in heaven. Give us this day our daily bread, and forgive us our trespasses, as we forgive those who trespass against us, and lead us not into temptation, but deliver us from evil. Amen.

Hail Mary, full of grace, the Lord is with you. Blessed are you among women, and blessed is the fruit of your womb, Jesus. Holy Mary, Mother of God, pray for us sinners, now and at the hour of our death. Amen.

Glory to the Father, and to the Son, and to the Holy Spirit, as it was in the beginning, is now, and will be forever. Amen.

For a Special Favor

St. Anthony, most gentle and kind saint of great virtue and charity toward all God's creatures, during your life on earth you were blessed with extraordinary gifts. Through your hands our compassionate Lord granted health to the sick; through your efforts he restored what was lost to those who were searching; through your words he granted solace to anguished hearts.

Encouraged by the power of your intercession, I come to you with complete confidence and implore you to obtain from the Lord what I now ask (*mention your request*).

The answer to my prayer may require a miracle; yet, are you not the saint of miracles? O gentle and loving St. Anthony, whose heart is ever full of human sympathy, take my prayer to the infant Jesus for whom you have such great love. Speak to him for me and the gratitude of my heart will ever be yours.

(*Our Father, Hail Mary, Glory to the Father....*)

Prayer to Recover Something Lost

St. Anthony intercedes for his devotees in the recovery of things that have been lost—material objects and, more importantly, immaterial things of the spirit. We can seek his intercession for those who have lost health, home, independence, faith, sobriety, virtue, a loved one, etc.

oving God, you have given us St. Anthony as an intercessor for those who have lost material objects and things of spiritual value. With confidence in his prayers before your throne, I recommend to his intercession what I have lost *(mention what has been lost)*. If it be according to your will and for my greater spiritual well-being, I ask that it be restored to me. I ask this and all things through your Son, Jesus Christ. Amen.

Prayer for One Who Has Lost Faith

ord Jesus, you are the Good Shepherd who takes care of his flock, always searching for and saving those who are lost. Grant that through the intercession of St. Anthony, all those who have lost their way in this world, especially *(mention friend or loved one)* may return to the life of faith given her/him in baptism. Although I do not understand, I believe that you still work in the lives of those who have wandered from the path of the Gospel, and that your unconditional love never ceases to reach out to them. Let me not lose hope, but continue to love and encourage *(name)* until the day she/he comes home to you. Amen.

Prayer for Special Graces

*H*oly Anthony, consolation of all who call upon you, encouraged by your promise to assist those who invoke you, I seek your intercession. With heartfelt sorrow for my sins, and trust in your prayers to God for me, I ask your help, your protection, your counsel, and your blessing. Obtain for me from God all the graces necessary for my spiritual welfare, and the particular favor I ask at this time *(mention your specific intention)*. Amen.

(Our Father, Hail Mary, Glory to the Father....)

V. Pray for us, St. Anthony,
R. That we may become worthy of the promises of Christ.

Let us pray.

Almighty and eternal God, you bestowed on your faithful confessor, Anthony, the gift of miraculous powers. In your mercy grant that what we seek through his merits we may receive through his intercession. We ask this through Jesus Christ your Son, our Lord. Amen.

Prayer of Praise and Thanksgiving

It is fitting for us to praise and thank God for the graces and privileges he has bestowed upon the saints. Devotees of St. Anthony of Padua may pray the following act of thanksgiving during their novena.

Lord Jesus, I praise, glorify, and bless you for all the graces and privileges you have bestowed upon your servant, St. Anthony, doctor, teacher, servant of the Gospel and the Church. By his merits grant me your grace, and through his intercession help me in all my needs. At the hour of my death be with me until that time when I can join the saints in heaven to praise you forever and ever. Amen.

Litany in Honor of St. Anthony

(For private use)

Lord, have mercy on us.
Christ, have mercy on us.
Christ, hear us.
Christ, graciously hear us.

Holy Mary, *pray for us.*
St. Francis of Assisi, *pray for us.*
St. Anthony of Padua, *pray for us.*
Glory of the Order of Friars Minor, *pray for us.*
Martyr in desiring to die for Christ, *pray for us.*
Pillar of the Church, *pray for us.*
Worthy priest of God, *pray for us.*
Apostolic preacher, *pray for us.*
Teacher of truth, *pray for us.*
Comforter of the afflicted, *pray for us.*
Helper in necessities, *pray for us.*
Deliverer of captives, *pray for us.*
Guide of the erring, *pray for us.*
Restorer of lost things, *pray for us.*
Chosen intercessor, *pray for us.*
Worker of miracles, *pray for us.*

Be merciful to us, spare us, O Lord.
Be merciful to us, hear us, O Lord.

From all evil, O Lord, *deliver us.*
From all sin, *deliver us.*
From all dangers of body and soul, *deliver us.*
From the deceits of Satan, *deliver us.*
From disease, hunger, and war, *deliver us.*
From eternal death, *deliver us.*
Through the merits of St. Anthony, *deliver us.*
Through his zeal for the conversion of sinners,
    deliver us.
Through his desire for the crown of martyrdom,
    deliver us.
Through his fatigues and labors, *deliver us.*
Through his preaching and teaching, *deliver us.*
Through his penitential tears, *deliver us.*
Through his patience and humility, *deliver us.*
Through his glorious death, *deliver us.*
In the day of judgment, *deliver us.*

That you lead us to true penance,
    we beseech you, hear us.
That you grant us patience in our trials,
    we beseech you, hear us.
That you assist us in our necessities,
    we beseech you, hear us.
That you grant our petitions,
    we beseech you, hear us.
That you kindle the fire of divine love within us,
    we beseech you, hear us.

That you grant us the protection and intercession
of St. Anthony, *we beseech you, hear us.*

Lamb of God, you take away the sins of the world,
spare us, O Lord.
Lamb of God, you take away the sins of the world,
graciously hear us, O Lord.
Lamb of God, you take away the sins of the world,
have mercy on us.
Christ, hear us.
Christ, graciously hear us.

V. Pray for us, St. Anthony.
R. That we may become worthy of the promises
of Christ.

Let us pray.

Almighty and eternal God, you bestowed on your
faithful confessor, Anthony, the gift of miraculous
powers. In your mercy grant that what we seek
through his merits we may receive through his intercession. We ask this through Jesus Christ your
Son, our Lord. Amen.

—Taken from common sources

Evening Prayer

*A*s this day draws to a close we place ourselves in an attitude of thanksgiving. We take time to express our gratitude to a loving God for his abiding presence. We thank him for the gift of the day and all it brought with it. We thank him for all the things we were able to achieve throughout the day, and we entrust to him the concerns we have for tomorrow.

From the rising to the setting of the sun,
    may the name of the Lord be praised.
Glory to the Father, and to the Son,
    and to the Holy Spirit,
as it was in the beginning, is now,
    and will be forever. Amen.

Take a few moments for a brief examination of conscience. Reflect on the ways God acted in your life today, how you responded to his invitations to think, speak, and act in a more Christ-like manner, and in what ways you would like to be a more faithful disciple tomorrow.

Lord, in your great love have mercy.

For the times I acted or spoke unkindly
  toward others.

Lord, have mercy.

For the times I was not generous with my time
  and talents.

Christ, have mercy.

For the times I was unwelcoming or unforgiving.

Lord, have mercy.

For the times… (any other petitions for pardon).
  (Or any other Act of Sorrow)

Psalm 104

May the glory of the Lord endure forever.

Bless the LORD, my soul.
LORD my God, how great you are.
You are robed in splendor and majesty,
clothed in light as a cloak,
You spread out the heavens like a tent,
set the timbers for your lodgings on the waters,
make the clouds your chariot,
and ride on the wings of the wind.

You establish the winds as your messengers,
flames of fire as your ministers,
and fixed the foundations of the earth
so that it shall not be moved for an eternity of
    eternities.
I will sing to the LORD as long as I live,
sing psalms to my God while I still have life.
May this meditation of mine be pleasing to him,
for I rejoice in the LORD.
Bless the LORD, my soul.

    Glory to the Father....

———————❧———————

The Word of God
John 12:24–26

    As followers of Jesus we are not all asked to give our physical lives for him or others. But the Lord does ask us to give who we are and share ourselves with others. When we give of ourselves freely—our time and talents—we experience true self-fulfillment, finding happiness here on earth and eternal joy in heaven.

*I*f the grain of wheat that falls to the ground
does not die, it remains alone.
But if it dies, it bears much fruit.
Whoever loves his life, loses it,

and whoever hates his life in this world,
will save it for eternal life.
If anyone would serve me, let him follow me,
and where I am, there will my servant be.
If anyone would serve me,
the Father will honor him.

Lord, you have the words of everlasting life.

In prayer we bring before the Lord our own needs and the needs of those we love. We take time to consider the needs of the world and intercede for those who do not or cannot pray. We offer petitions for the improvement of the human condition so that our world will be a better place to live, and all people may contribute to building up God's kingdom here on earth.

Intercessions

*G*racious and loving God, we come before you at the close of this day to present the needs of your people.

Response: *Lord, hear our prayer through the intercession of St. Anthony.*

For Church leaders and those who minister in your name: may they lead lives of holiness and seek to be true witnesses to the Gospel message of love and compassion. **R.**

For world leaders: may they govern with integrity and justice, so that the peoples of every nation may live in peace and dignity. **R.**

For those who have lost loved ones as a result of violence: may they know the comfort of a loving God and the support of the human family. **R.**

For those who have lost faith: may they receive the strength and encouragement to welcome the Lord back into their lives. **R.**

For all those who suffer in body, mind, or spirit (*especially N.*): may they know the healing touch of the Divine Physician. **R.**

For those who are terminally ill (*especially N.*): may they walk hand in hand with God to receive comfort and strength in their pain, fear, and anxiety. **R.**

For those who have died (*especially N.*): may they soon enjoy light, happiness, and peace in the joy of heaven. **R.**

(*Add your own general intentions and your particular intentions for this novena.*)

Conclude your intercession by praying to our Heavenly Father in the words Jesus taught us:

Our Father....

Closing Prayer

*G*racious and loving God, as evening falls and this day draws to a close, remain with us. Guard us from evil and bring us safely through the night so that with the coming of the dawn we may give you praise and serve you more faithfully. We ask this through Jesus Christ, your Son. Amen.

Mary, Jesus' Mother and ours, is always ready to intercede for those who ask her help.

Remember, O most gracious Virgin Mary, that never was it known that anyone who fled to your protection, implored your help, or sought your intercession, was left unaided. Inspired with this confidence, I fly to you, O Virgin of virgins, my Mother; to you I come; before you I kneel, sinful and sorrowful. O Mother of the Word Incarnate, despise not my petitions, but in your mercy hear and answer me. Amen.

May God's blessing remain with us forever. In the name of the Father, and of the Son, and of the Holy Spirit. Amen.

BOOKS & MEDIA

The Daughters of St. Paul operate book and media centers at the following addresses. Visit, call, or write the one nearest you today, or find us at www.paulinestore.org.

CALIFORNIA
3908 Sepulveda Blvd, Culver City, CA 90230   310-397-8676
3250 Middlefield Road, Menlo Park, CA 94025   650-562-7060

FLORIDA
145 S.W. 107th Avenue, Miami, FL 33174   305-559-6715

HAWAII
1143 Bishop Street, Honolulu, HI 96813   808-521-2731

ILLINOIS
172 North Michigan Avenue, Chicago, IL 60601   312-346-4228

LOUISIANA
4403 Veterans Memorial Blvd, Metairie, LA 70006   504-887-7631

MASSACHUSETTS
885 Providence Hwy, Dedham, MA 02026   781-326-5385

MISSOURI
9804 Watson Road, St. Louis, MO 63126   314-965-3512

NEW YORK
115 E. 29th Street, New York City, NY 10016   212-754-1110

SOUTH CAROLINA
243 King Street, Charleston, SC 29401   843-577-0175

TEXAS
No book center; for parish exhibits or outreach evangelization, contact: 210-569-0500, or SanAntonio@paulinemedia.com, or P.O. Box 761416, San Antonio, TX 78245

VIRGINIA
1025 King Street, Alexandria, VA 22314   703-549-3806

CANADA
3022 Dufferin Street, Toronto, ON M6B 3T5   416-781-9131